First Friends 2

Activity Book

Susan Iannuzzi

OXFORD
UNIVERSITY PRESS

Level 2 Scope and sequence

Topic	Structure	Vocabulary	Letters and phonics	Numbers	Songs and chants
1 Hello	Revision I'm (name). Commands	Revision Days of the week	Alphabet revision	**Revision:** 1–2 **Number words:** one, two	**Lesson 2:** Days of the week **Lesson 3:** Letter song **Lesson 4:** Letter song
2 Our school	What's this? It's… Who's this? He's… / She's…	classroom friend music room playground sandbox school bus seesaw teacher	Alphabet revision	**Revision:** 3–5 **Number words:** three, four, five	
3 My friends	Are you…? Yes, I am. / No, I'm not.	cold happy hot hungry sad thirsty tired	**digraph 'sh'** sheep shoes fish	**Revision:** 6–8 **Number words:** six, seven, eight	**Lesson 3:** Letter song **Lesson 4:** If you're happy…
4 I can…	I can…	catch climb draw jump kick run sing throw	**digraph 'th'** throw thumb bath	**Revision:** 9–10 **Number words:** nine, ten	**Lesson 3:** Letter song **Lesson 4:** I can jump…
5 My home	There is… / There are…	bedroom dining room kitchen living room lamp plant sofa TV	**digraph 'ch'** chocolate beach kitchen	11–12 eleven, twelve	**Lesson 3:** Letter song **Lesson 4:** Bean plant, bean plant, Grow, grow, grow

Topic	Structure	Vocabulary	Letters and phonics	Numbers	Songs and chants
6 My room	Where is it? It's in / on / under…	bed blanket shelf pillow wardrobe in on under	**CVC with 'a':** cat hat mat	13–14 thirteen, fourteen	**Lesson 3:** Letter song **Lesson 4:** Put your hand on your head
7 On holiday	How many are there? There are…	beach crab sand sandcastle sea shell umbrella black brown purple white	**CVC with 'e':** jet net wet	15–16 fifteen, sixteen	**Lesson 3:** Letter song **Lesson 4:** Ten umbrellas in the sun
8 Mealtime	She / He's got…	cheese chicken fish juice potato rice salad soup	**CVC with 'i':** big dig fig	17–18 seventeen, eighteen	**Lesson 3:** Letter song **Lesson 4:** I love food, let's eat, please
9 Circus fun	She / He / It can…	acrobat bicycle clown drum juggler parrot tent	**CVC with 'o':** hop mop top	19–20 nineteen, twenty	**Lesson 3:** Letter song **Lesson 4:** Let's all go to the circus
10 Jobs	Is she / he…? Yes, she / he is. / No, she / he isn't.	builder doctor farmer fireman policeman secretary shop assistant (taxi) driver	**CVC with 'u':** bun run sun	Numbers 11–20 – revision	**Lesson 3:** Letter song **Lesson 4:** How are you today? **Lesson 5:** Twenty horses on the farm

1 Hello

1 Trace and colour.

2 Draw yourself. Write and say.

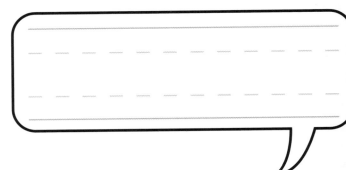

1 Trace and say. Draw.

Sunday	
Monday	
Tuesday	
Wednesday	
Thursday	
Friday	
Saturday	

1 Trace and match.

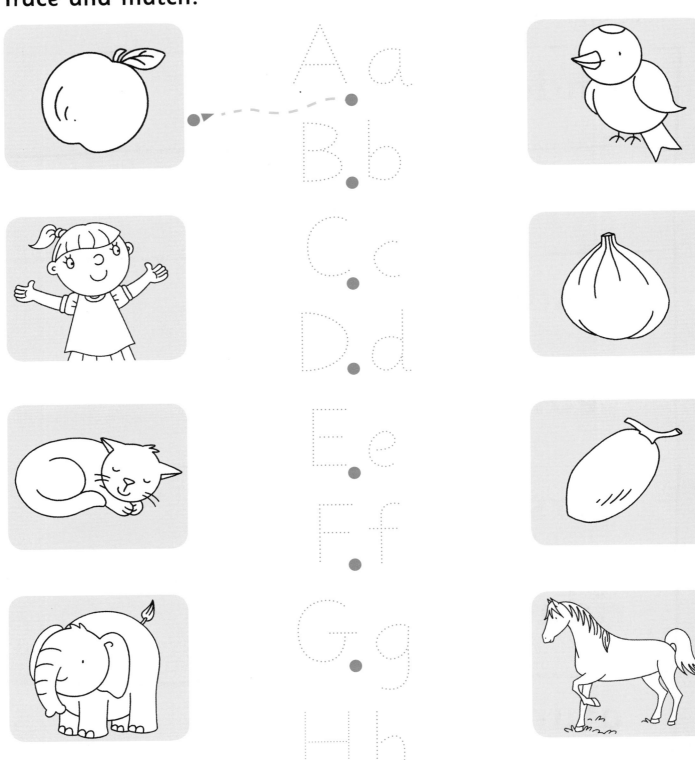

1 Trace and match.

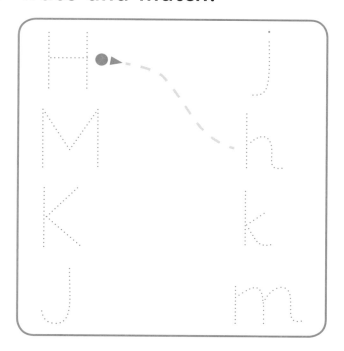

2 Write.

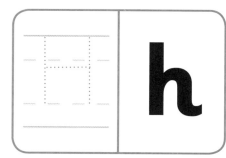
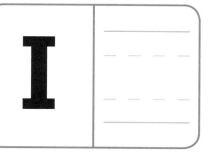
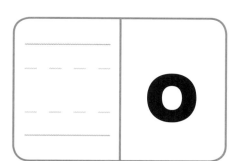

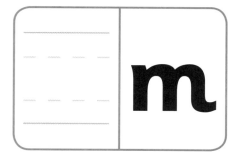

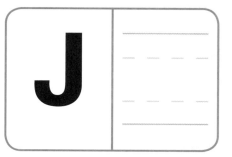

1 Count, trace and write.

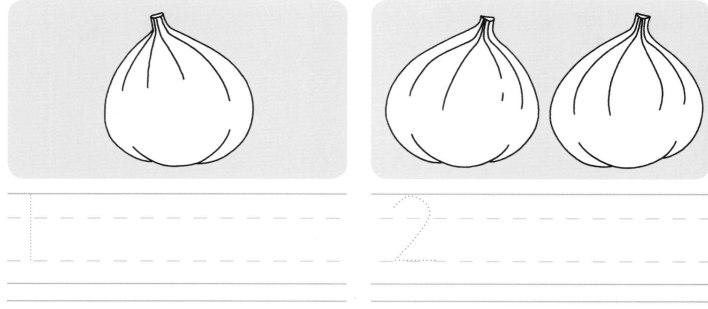

2 Read and draw.

one cat

two birds

1 Match and say.

Unit 1 Review

1 Say and write.

a   b   c

i

f   g

m   o

l

2 Match.

1 • - - - - → **one**

2   **two**

2 Our school

1 Match and say.

 music room

sandbox

 playground

school bus

 teacher

classroom

 seesaw

friend

1 Say and match.

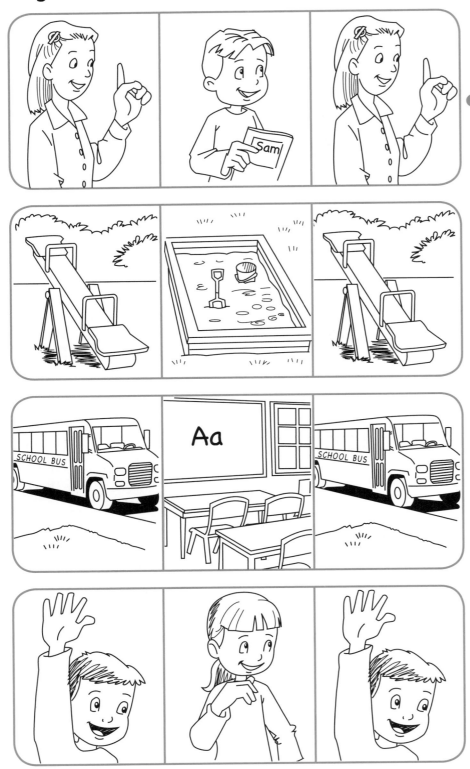

1 Say and write.

Pp Qq Rr Ss Tt Uu

s

1 Trace and match.

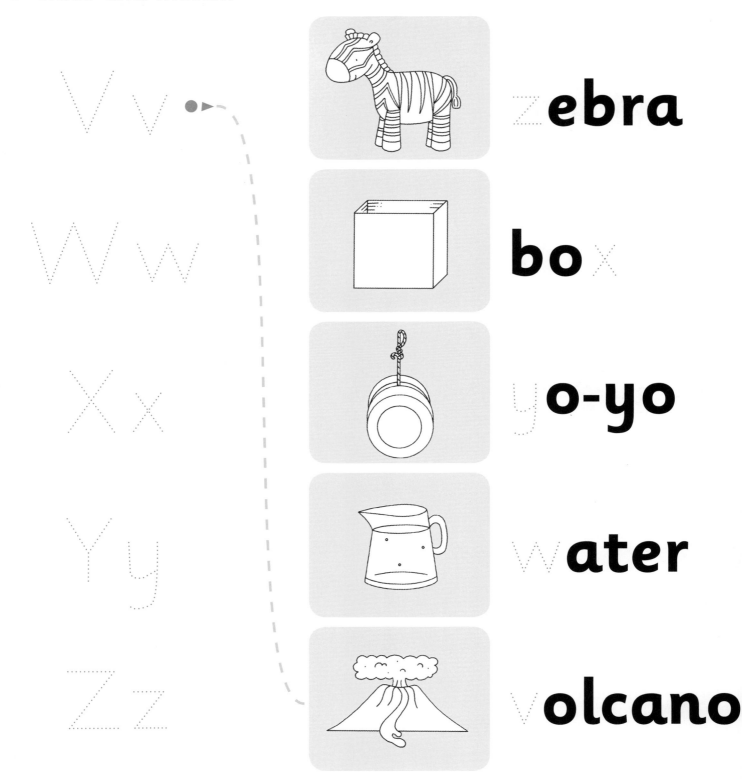

V v

W w

X x

Y y

Z z

zebra

bo x

o-yo

ater

olcano

1 Trace and write. Count and colour.

2 Trace and write.

three

four

five

1 Circle.

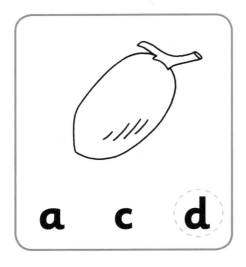

a   c   d

t   f   p

b   l   k

s   h   u

n   u   v

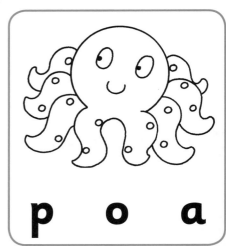

p   o   a

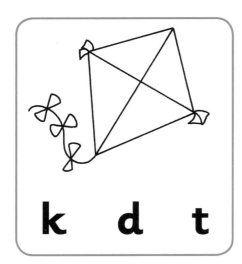

k   d   t

s   f   w

n   u   c

1 Say and write.

n   o   p

r   w   t

y

2 Count and circle.

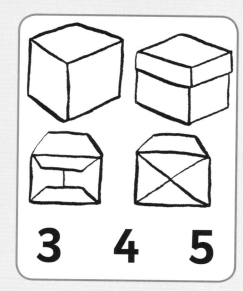

3   4   5

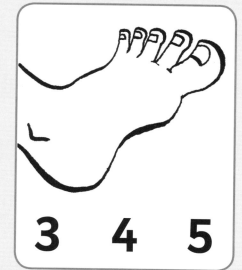

3   4   5

3   4   5

3 My friends

1 Circle and say.

	tired	cold	happy
	sad	hot	hungry
	cold	tired	thirsty
	happy	hot	hungry
	tired	sad	thirsty
	hot	cold	happy

1 Match and write.

happy

tired

sad

hungry

I'm _____ .

I'm _____ .

I'm _____ .

I'm _____ .

1 Circle *sh*. Trace and write.

2 Write and say.

fi _____

_____ oes

1 Colour the *sh* fish.

2 Colour the pictures with the *sh* sound.

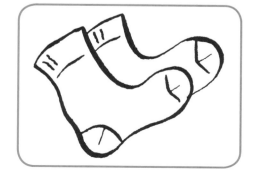

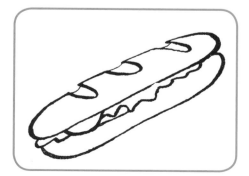

1 Trace and match.

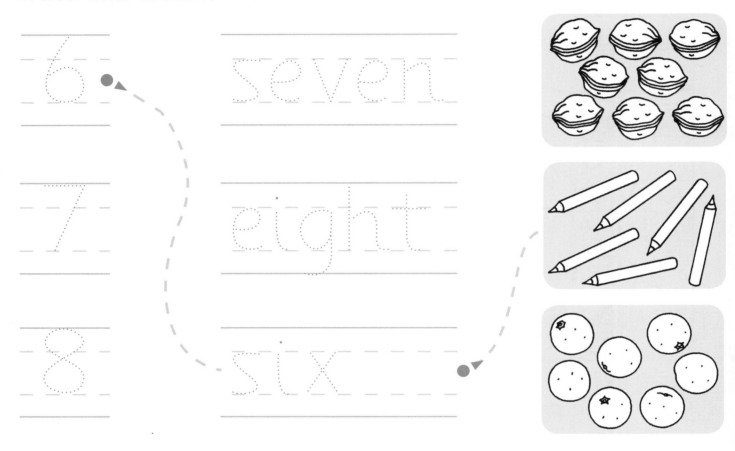

2 Count and circle.

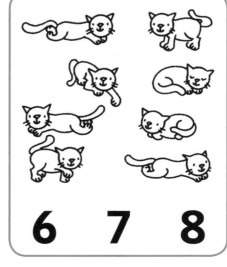

1 Read and write.   **Yes   No**

Are you cold?

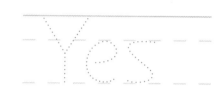

Are you thirsty?

Are you hot?

Are you sad?

1 Say and write.

_____**eep** **fi**_____

2 Count and match.

six

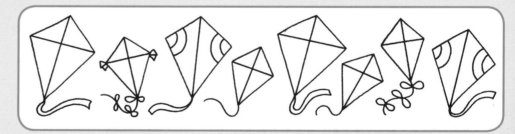

seven

eight

4 I can...

1 Match and say.

run

climb

jump

draw

kick

catch

throw

sing

1 Write and draw.　　**catch throw jump climb**

I can _____ .

I can't _____ .

1 Circle *th*. Trace and write.

thumb

bath

th th th

2 Write and say.

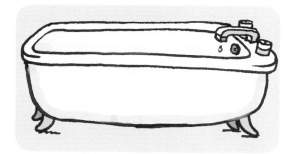

ba

  row

1 Circle.

th

sh

t

s

th

1 Count, trace and write.

9 _____ nine _____

10 _____ ten _____

2 Join the dots.

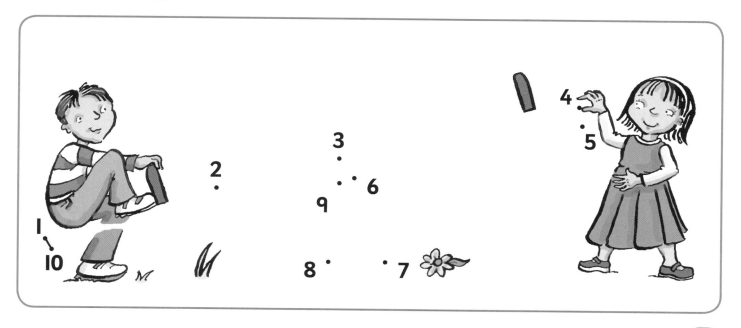

1 Count and colour. Trace.

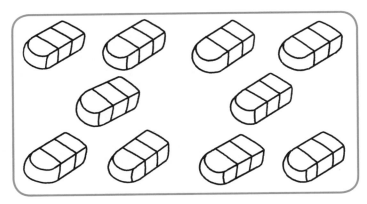

nine

ten

eight

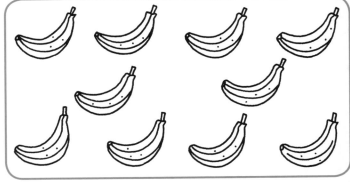

five

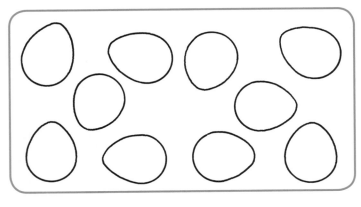

seven

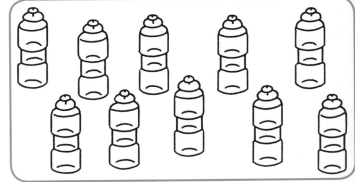

two

1 Match.

bath

throw

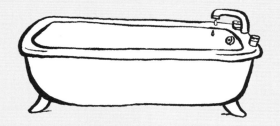

thumb

2 Count and write.

t _____

n _____

5 My home

1 Match and circle.

plant

living room

dining room

sofa

plant

kitchen

living room

lamp

dining room

living room

plant

TV

1 Read and draw.

bedroom	**dining room**

2 Draw and say.

My home.

1 Circle *ch*. Trace and write.

chocolate

beach

ch ch ch

2 Write and say.

air

kit   en

1 Say and circle.

ch   sh

ch   sh

ch   sh

ch   sh

ch   sh

ch   sh

ch   sh

ch   sh

ch   sh

1 Count, trace and write.

11 _____ 12 _____

eleven twelve

2 Write the words.   **eleven four two seven ten eight**

one _____   **three** _____

five   six _____   _____

nine _____   **twelve**

1 Look, read and circle.

There's a sofa.	Yes	No
There's a TV.	Yes	No
There's a chair.	Yes	No
There's a lamp.	Yes	No
There's a plant.	Yes	No
There's a table.	Yes	No
There's a doll.	Yes	No

1 Circle the pictures with the *ch* sound.

2 Count and circle. Write.

11　　　12

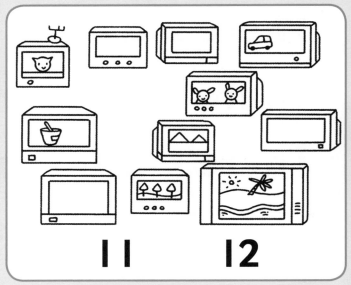

11　　　12

t

e

6 My room

1 Write and say.

bed   blanket   shelf
pillow   wardrobe

1 Trace and match.

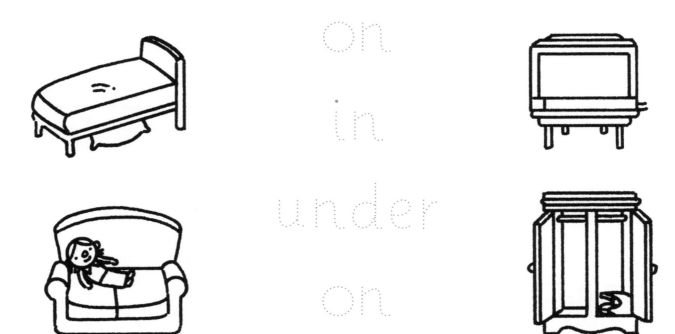

2 Write. Ask and answer.

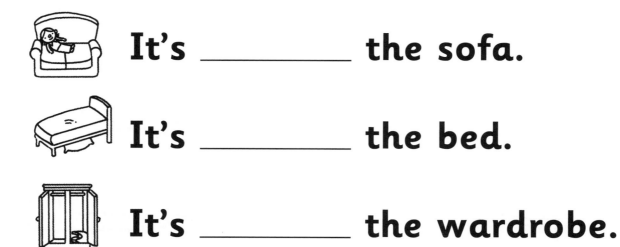

It's _____ the sofa.

It's _____ the bed.

It's _____ the wardrobe.

It's _____ the table.

1 Trace and write.

at at

2 Write and say.

    **at**

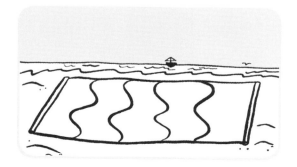    **at**

1 Read and match.

A cat under a mat.

A hat on a cat.

A cat in a hat.

2 Read and draw.

A cat on a mat.

1 Count, trace and write.

13 _____ 14 _____

thirteen   fourteen

2 Count and match.

13

fourteen

14

thirteen

1 Look, read and write.

| in on under | sofa coat blanket |

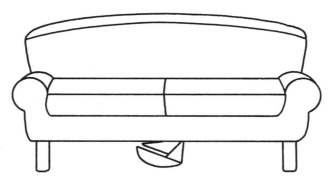

The boat is _____ **the** _____ **.**

The boat is _____ **the** _____ **.**

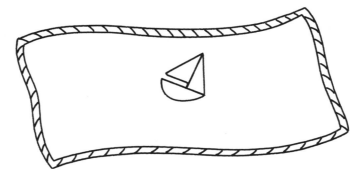

The boat is _____ **the** _____ **.**

1 Look and circle.

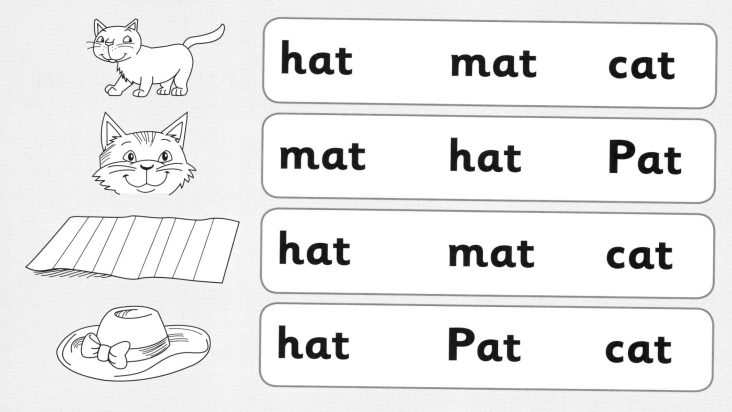

	hat	mat	cat
	mat	hat	Pat
	hat	mat	cat
	hat	Pat	cat

2 Read, colour and say.

thirteen pillows

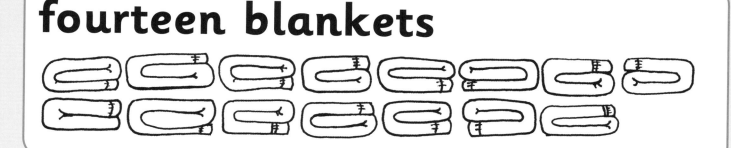

fourteen blankets

7 On holiday

1 Write and say.

> umbrella   shell   crab
> beach   sandcastle   sea

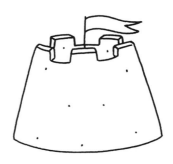

1 Count and write.

 2

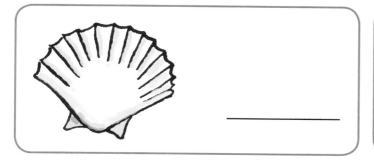

1 Trace and write.

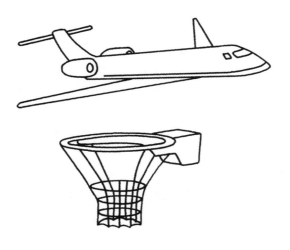

et et

2 Write and say.

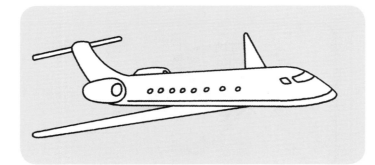

t   j   e

_____ _____ _____

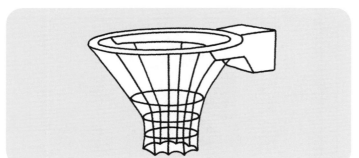

e   t   n

_____ _____ _____

1 Colour.

(1 yellow) (2 blue) (3 red) (4 green) (5 orange)

(6 pink) (7 purple) (8 black) (9 brown)

1 Count, trace and write.

15

fifteen

16

sixteen

2 Read and colour.

15 brown nuts

16 blue pens

13 yellow shells

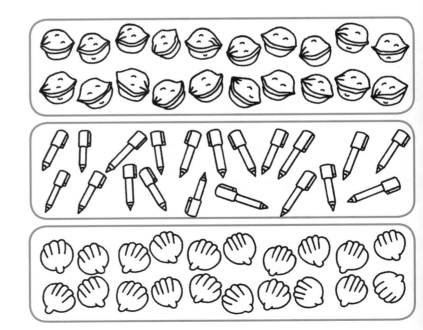

1 Join the dots.

2 Look, read and write.

How many sandcastles are there?

There are _____ sandcastles.

1 Say and write.

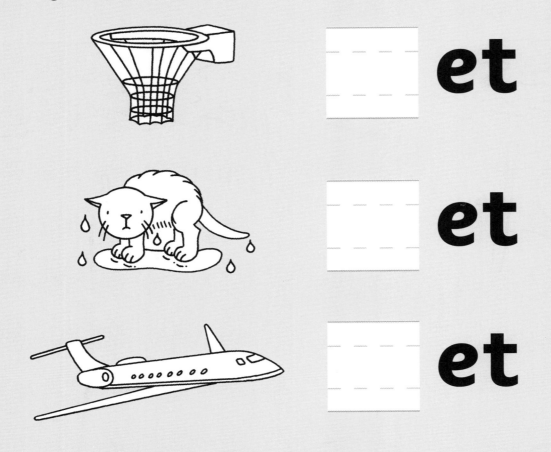

et

et

et

2 Count and write.

| fifteen | sixteen |

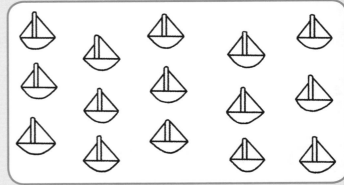

1 Match.

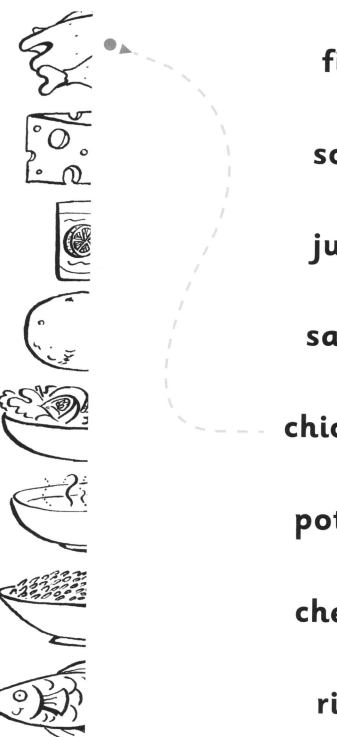

fish

soup

juice

salad

chicken

potato

cheese

rice

1 Look, read and write.

chicken salad soup fish cheese rice

She's got

_____, _____

and _____ .

He's got

_____, _____

and _____ .

2 Draw and say.

I've got ...

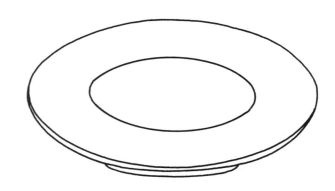

1 Trace and write.

ig ig

2 Write and say.

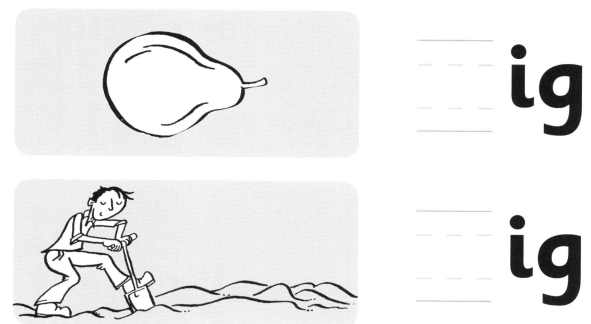

ig

ig

1 Circle.

dig   bin

hat   mat

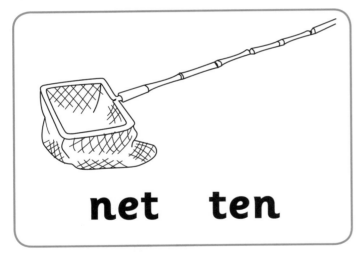

net   ten

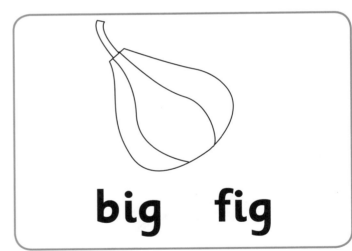

big   fig

Pat   pen

Jig   jet

1 Count, trace and write.

17

18

seventeen eighteen

2 Count and match.

eleven

thirteen

seventeen

eighteen

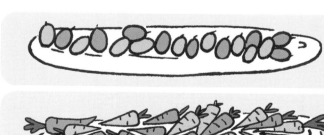

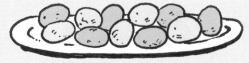

1 Say and match the rhyming words.

1 Say and write.

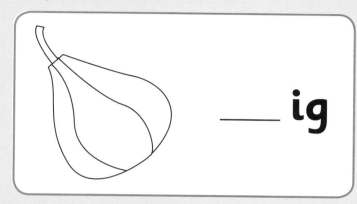 ___ **ig**

 ___ **ig**

 ___ **ig**

 ___ **ig**

2 Count and write.

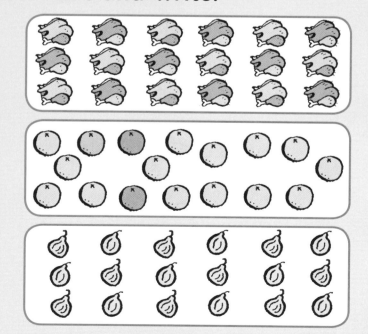

___ **chickens**

___ **oranges**

___ **figs**

9 Circus fun

Lesson 1

1 Write and say.

acrobat bicycle clown tent drum juggler parrot

_____

_____

_____

_____

_____ _____ and _____

1 Read and circle.

 She can sing.   Yes   **No**

 He can climb.   Yes   No

 She can jump.   Yes   No

 He can catch.   Yes   No

2 Write and draw.

I can _____ .

1 Trace and write.

op op

2 Write and say.

o   p   h

___ ___ ___

p   o   m

___ ___ ___

1 Read and draw.

The clown can play a drum.

2 Find and colour.

op op at ig

at ig et at

et at op et

ig et op ig

1 Count, trace and write.

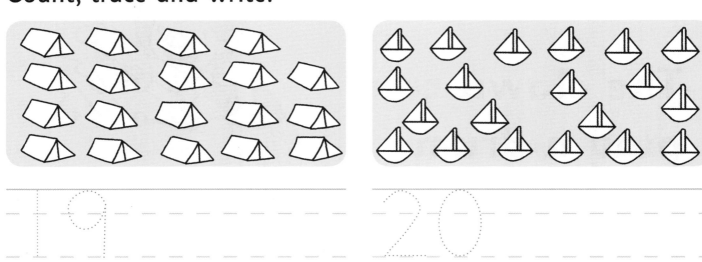

19 nineteen

20 twenty

2 Read and colour.

nineteen blue drums

twenty green parrots

1 Read and match. Write the number.

1 She can draw.

2 He can't climb.

3 She can't run.

4 He can catch.

5 She can kick.

1 Say and write.

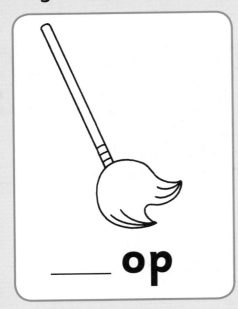

___op

___op

___op

2 Count and write.   **nineteen   twenty**

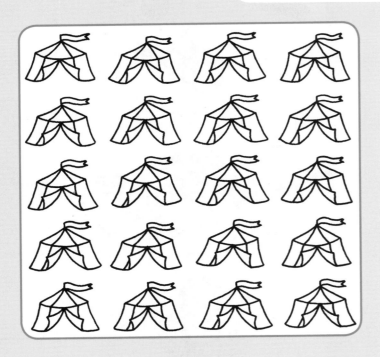

_____   _____

10 Jobs

1 Write and trace.

 __ octor

 __ armer

 __ ecretary

 __ oliceman

 __ uilder

1 Circle and say.

policeman
fireman

doctor
builder

acrobat
teacher

shop assistant
taxi driver

clown
juggler

school bus driver
shop assistant

1 Trace and write.

un un

2 Write and say.

un

un

Lesson 4

1 Look and circle the letters. Read.

hat	man	sad
dad	bag	Baz

jet	Tess	bed
tent	red	egg

big	six	fig
Jig	bin	in

box	hop	on
mop	top	dog

under	sun	jump
bun	nut	mum

1 Join the dots.

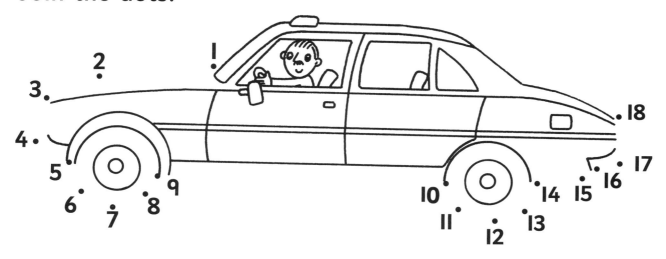

He's a taxi driver.

2 Join the dots and write.

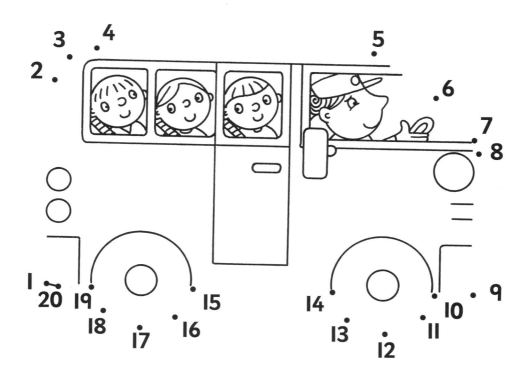

She's a _____ _____ driver.

1 Read and circle.

 He is a fireman.   Yes   No

 He is a farmer.   Yes   No

 She is a secretary.   Yes   No

 He is a builder.   Yes   No

 She is a juggler.   Yes   No

 She is a teacher.   Yes   No

1 Circle the pictures with the *un* sound.

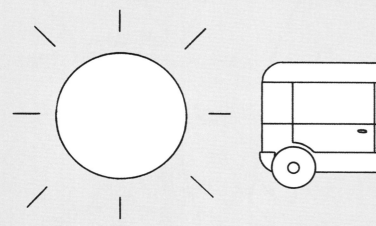 

2 Write the numbers.

12   15

16   19

Numbers

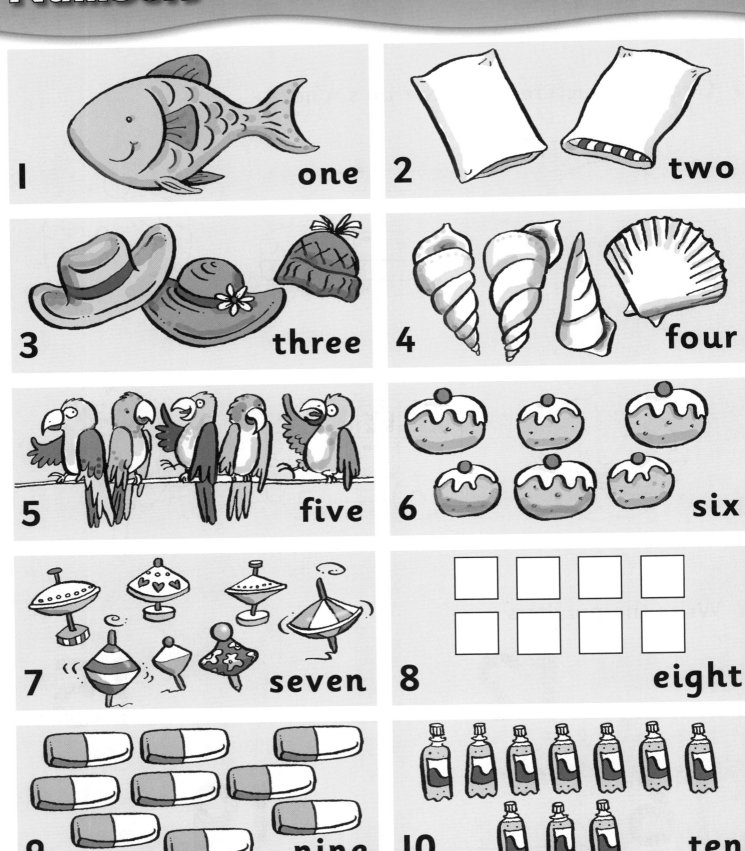

1 one

2 two

3 three

4 four

5 five

6 six

7 seven

8 eight

9 nine

10 ten

11 eleven

12 twelve

13 thirteen

14 fourteen

15 fifteen

16 sixteen

17 seventeen

18 eighteen

19 nineteen

20 twenty

Writing grid

Make a beach umbrella

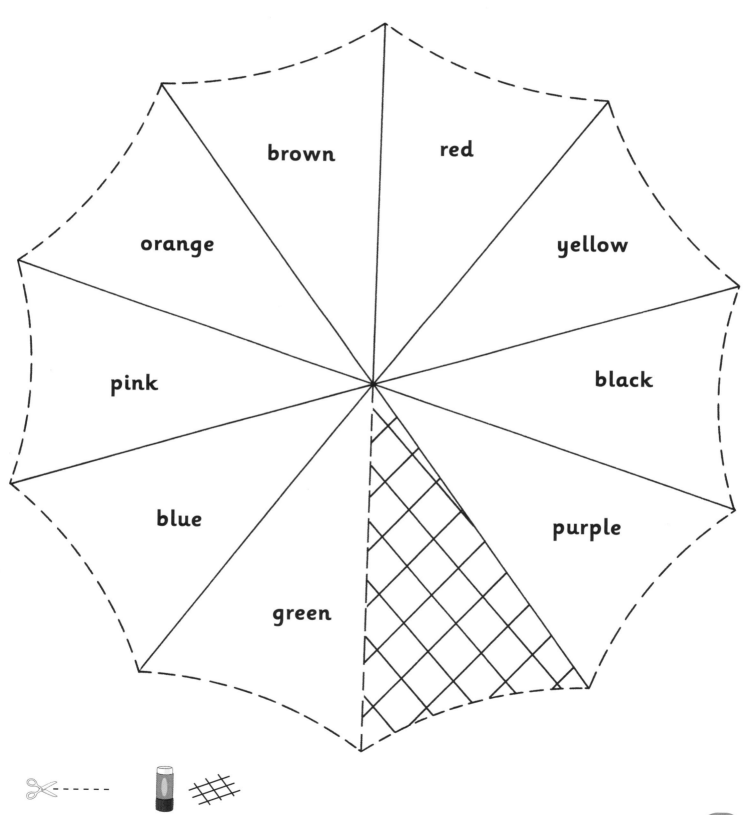

brown

red

orange

yellow

pink

black

blue

purple

green

1 Colour, cut out and glue the template to make your umbrella.
2 Attach your umbrella to a stick, pencil or straw, using sticky tape or modelling clay.

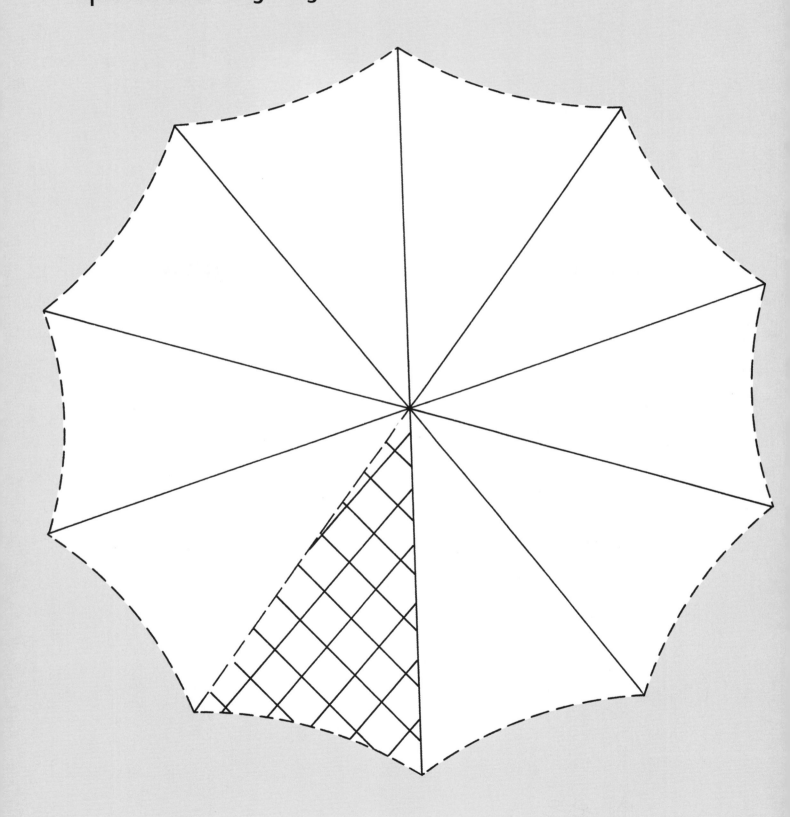

Songs

Unit 1
Lesson 2

Sunday, Monday, Tuesday, Wednesday,
Thursday, Friday, Saturday
It's a nice day!
It's Monday.

Unit 3
Lesson 4

If you're happy and you know it,
clap your hands.
If you're happy and you know it,
clap your hands.
If you're happy and you know it,
and you really want to show it
If you're happy and you know it,
clap your hands.

If you're sad and you know it,
stamp your feet.
If you're sad and you know it,
stamp your feet.
If you're sad and you know it,
and you really want to show it
If you're sad and you know it,
stamp your feet.

Unit 4
Lesson 4

I can jump
I can climb
I can sing and count to five.

I can throw
I can kick
I can catch and run and hide.

Unit 5
Lesson 4

Bean plant, bean plant
Grow, grow, grow!
Water and sun
Grow, grow, grow!

Unit 6
Lesson 4

Put your hand on your head.
Put your hand on your nose.
Put your hand on your leg.
Put your hand on your toes.

Put your hand in your bag.
Put your hand in the air.
Put your hand under your book.
Shake your hands everywhere.

Unit 7
Lesson 4

Ten umbrellas in the sun.
There's a colour for everyone.
Black, white, brown, blue.
Green for me; purple for you.
Yellow, orange, pink, and red.
Sun is shining.
Hide your head!

Unit 8
Lesson 4

Salad and soup
Chicken and cheese
I love food!
Let's eat, please!

Fish and potatoes
Juice and rice
I love food!
Yummy! It's nice.

Unit 9
Lesson 4

(Chorus)

Let's all go to the circus.
Let's all go to the circus.
Let's all go to the circus.
What can you see?

I can see an acrobat.
I can see an acrobat.
I can see an acrobat.
He can jump and climb.

(Chorus)

I can see a juggler.
I can see a juggler.
I can see a juggler.
She can throw and catch.

(Chorus)

I can see a clown.
I can see a clown.
I can see a clown.
He can play a drum.

Unit 10
Lesson 4

How are you today?
How are you today?

I'm not very well.
Is the doctor on the way?

How are you today?
How are you today?

Thanks to the doctor.
I can play!

Unit 10
Lesson 5

Twenty horses on the farm.
EE-I-EE-I-O
Twenty horses on the farm.
Oh, no! One must go.

Nineteen horses on the farm.
EE-I-EE-I-O
Nineteen horses on the farm.
Oh, no! One must go.

...

One horse on the farm.
EE-I-EE-I-O
One horse on the farm.
Oh, no! One must go.

OXFORD
UNIVERSITY PRESS

Great Clarendon Street, Oxford OX2 6DP

Oxford University Press is a department of the University of Oxford.
It furthers the University's objective of excellence in research, scholarship,
and education by publishing worldwide in

Oxford New York

Auckland Cape Town Dar es Salaam Hong Kong Karachi
Kuala Lumpur Madrid Melbourne Mexico City Nairobi
New Delhi Shanghai Taipei Toronto

With offices in

Argentina Austria Brazil Chile Czech Republic France Greece
Guatemala Hungary Italy Japan Poland Portugal Singapore
South Korea Switzerland Thailand Turkey Ukraine Vietnam

OXFORD and OXFORD ENGLISH are registered trade marks of
Oxford University Press in the UK and in certain other countries

ISBN: 978 0 19 443211 5

Printed in China

This book is printed on paper from certified and well-managed sources.

ACKNOWLEDGEMENTS

Illustrations by: Paul Gibbs and John Haslam pp 4, 9, 11, 12, 13, 45 (top), 56, 59
(top), 70; Cathy Hughes pp 6, 8, 14, 16, 18, 20, 22, 24, 28, 30, 32, 34, 36, 38, 40,
42, 44, 46, 48, 50, 52, 54, 58, 60, 62, 64, 66, 68, 71, 73, 77, 78; Lisa Williams/
Sylvie Poggio Artists Agency pp 5, 10, 15, 17, 19, 21, 23, 25, 27, 29, 31, 33, 35,
37, 39, 41, 43, 45 (bottom), 47, 49, 51, 53, 55, 57, 59 (bottom), 61, 63, 65, 67,
69, 72, 74, 75.